ISBN: 979-8-9856174-1-2
(PAPERBACK)

First Edition 2022
First Printing 2022

Printed in the United States of American

Welcome & Thank you

Congratulations!
Self-Care is important and you have taken a step forward by purchasing this journal. I commend you for understanding how important your well-being is. You have made yourself a priority. Doing so not only benefits you, but the people you love as well. The people who love you and depend on you would much rather see you positive, full of energy and happy, than tired and unhappy.
This Journal will help to equip you with the tools to make self-care
an ongoing part of your life's journey.

Thank you for choosing our journal to assist you in your journey.

Moreen Jordan, M.A., L.P.C.
Marital & Family Therapist

THIS BOOK BELONGS TO

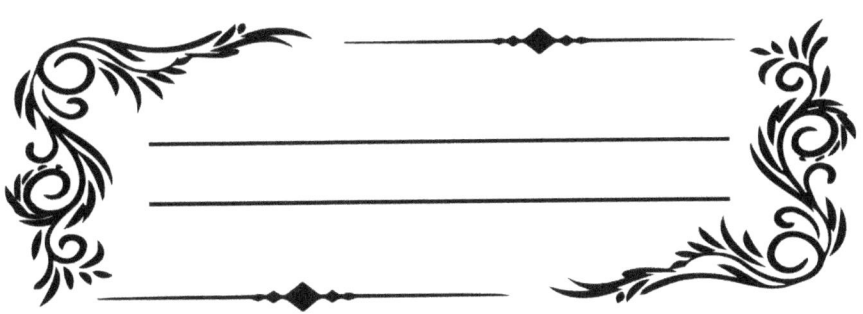

JOURNEY

MONTH: ....

YEAR: ....

ACTS OF SELF-CARE

_____   _____
_____   _____
_____   _____

AFFIRMATION

- ☐
- ☐
- ☐
- ☐

TODAY'S MOOD

☹ ☹ 😐 🙂 😃

I'M GRATEFUL FOR

INSPIRATION: ....
....
....

JOURNEY

MONTH: ....

YEAR: ....

ACTS OF SELF-CARE

_____   _____
_____   _____
_____   _____

AFFIRMATION

■
■
■
■

TODAY'S MOOD

☹ ☹ 😐 ☺ 😄

I'M GRATEFUL FOR

INSPIRATION: ....
....
....

JOURNEY

MONTH: ....

YEAR: ....

ACTS OF SELF-CARE

_____   _____

_____   _____

_____   _____

AFFIRMATION

- ☐
- ☐
- ☐
- ☐

TODAY'S MOOD

☹ ☹ 😐 ☺ 😀

I'M GRATEFUL FOR

INSPIRATION: ....

....

....

 *Self Care*

JOURNEY

MONTH: ....

YEAR: ....

ACTS OF SELF-CARE

_____   _____
_____   _____
_____   _____

AFFIRMATION

■

■

■

■

TODAY'S MOOD

☹ ☹ 😐 🙂 😃

I'M GRATEFUL FOR

INSPIRATION: ....
....
....

JOURNEY

MONTH: ....

YEAR: ....

ACTS OF SELF-CARE

_____   _____
_____   _____
_____   _____

AFFIRMATION

-
-
-
-

TODAY'S MOOD

☹ ☹ 😐 ☺ 😄

I'M GRATEFUL FOR

INSPIRATION: ....
....
....

JOURNEY

MONTH: ....

YEAR: ....

ACTS OF SELF-CARE

_____   _____

_____   _____

_____   _____

AFFIRMATION

- ☐
- ☐
- ☐
- ☐

TODAY'S MOOD

☹ ☹ 😐 ☺ 😃

I'M GRATEFUL FOR

INSPIRATION: ....

....

....

Self Care
JOURNEY

MONTH: ....

YEAR: ....

ACTS OF SELF-CARE

_____   _____

_____   _____

_____   _____

AFFIRMATION

- ▪
- ▪
- ▪
- ▪

TODAY'S MOOD

☹ ☹ 😐 ☺ 😃

I'M GRATEFUL FOR

INSPIRATION: ....

....

....

JOURNEY

MONTH: ....

YEAR: ....

ACTS OF SELF-CARE

_____   _____

_____   _____

_____   _____

AFFIRMATION

- ☐
- ☐
- ☐
- ☐

TODAY'S MOOD

☹ ☹ 😐 🙂 😄

I'M GRATEFUL FOR

INSPIRATION: ....

....

....

 *Self Care*

JOURNEY

MONTH: ....

YEAR: ....

ACTS OF SELF-CARE

_____   _____

_____   _____

_____   _____

AFFIRMATION

- ▪
- ▪
- ▪
- ▪

TODAY'S MOOD

I'M GRATEFUL FOR

INSPIRATION: ....

....

....

Self Care
JOURNEY

MONTH: ....

YEAR: ....

ACTS OF SELF-CARE

_____   _____

_____   _____

_____   _____

AFFIRMATION

- ▪
- ▪
- ▪
- ▪

TODAY'S MOOD

☹ ☹ 😐 ☺ 😀

I'M GRATEFUL FOR

INSPIRATION: ....

....

....

JOURNEY

MONTH: ....

YEAR: ....

ACTS OF SELF-CARE

_____ _____

_____ _____

_____ _____

AFFIRMATION

- ■
- ■
- ■
- ■

TODAY'S MOOD

☹ ☹ 😐 🙂 😃

I'M GRATEFUL FOR

INSPIRATION: ....

....

....

JOURNEY

MONTH: ....

YEAR: ....

ACTS OF SELF-CARE

_____   _____
_____   _____
_____   _____

AFFIRMATION

- ▪
- ▪
- ▪
- ▪

TODAY'S MOOD

☹ ☹ 😐 ☺ 😀

I'M GRATEFUL FOR

INSPIRATION: ....

....

....

JOURNEY

MONTH: ....

YEAR: ....

ACTS OF SELF-CARE

_____ _____

_____ _____

_____ _____

AFFIRMATION

☐

☐

☐

☐

TODAY'S MOOD

☹ ☹ 😐 ☺ 😀

I'M GRATEFUL FOR

INSPIRATION: ....

....

....

JOURNEY

MONTH: ....

YEAR: ....

ACTS OF SELF-CARE

_____   _____
_____   _____
_____   _____

AFFIRMATION

- ▪
- ▪
- ▪
- ▪

TODAY'S MOOD

☹ ☹ 😐 ☺ 😃

I'M GRATEFUL FOR

INSPIRATION: ....
....
....

Self Care
JOURNEY

MONTH: ....

YEAR: ....

ACTS OF SELF-CARE

_____   _____
_____   _____
_____   _____

AFFIRMATION

- ▪
- ▪
- ▪
- ▪

TODAY'S MOOD

I'M GRATEFUL FOR

INSPIRATION: ....
....
....

JOURNEY

MONTH: ....

YEAR: ....

ACTS OF SELF-CARE

_____   _____

_____   _____

_____   _____

AFFIRMATION

- ▪
- ▪
- ▪
- ▪

TODAY'S MOOD

☹ 😦 😐 🙂 😄

I'M GRATEFUL FOR

INSPIRATION: ....

....

....

Self Care
PLANNER

MONTH: ....

YEAR: ....

MY TOP PRIORITIES

GOALS FOR MY MIND:

- _____
- _____
- _____
- _____

GOALS FOR MY BODY:

- _____
- _____
- _____
- _____

REMINDER

MY NOTE

PLANNER

MONTH: ....

YEAR: ....

MY TOP PRIORITIES

GOALS FOR
MY MIND:

- _____
- _____
- _____
- _____

GOALS FOR
MY BODY:

- _____
- _____
- _____
- _____

REMINDER

MY NOTE

PLANNER

MONTH: ....

YEAR: ....

MY TOP PRIORITIES

GOALS FOR MY MIND:

- ◾ _____
- ◾ _____
- ◾ _____
- ◾ _____

GOALS FOR MY BODY:

- ◾ _____
- ◾ _____
- ◾ _____
- ◾ _____

REMINDER

MY NOTE

PLANNER

MONTH: ....

YEAR: ....

MY TOP PRIORITIES

GOALS FOR MY MIND:

- ☐ _____
- ☐ _____
- ☐ _____
- ☐ _____

GOALS FOR MY BODY:

- ☐ _____
- ☐ _____
- ☐ _____
- ☐ _____

REMINDER

MY NOTE

Self Care
PLANNER

MONTH: ....

YEAR: ....

MY TOP PRIORITIES

GOALS FOR MY MIND:

- ▪ _____
- ▪ _____
- ▪ _____
- ▪ _____

GOALS FOR MY BODY:

- ▪ _____
- ▪ _____
- ▪ _____
- ▪ _____

REMINDER

MY NOTE

 *Self Care*

PLANNER

MONTH: ....

YEAR: ....

MY TOP PRIORITIES

GOALS FOR MY MIND:

- _____
- _____
- _____
- _____

GOALS FOR MY BODY:

- _____
- _____
- _____
- _____

REMINDER

MY NOTE

PLANNER

MONTH: ....

YEAR: ....

MY TOP PRIORITIES

GOALS FOR MY MIND:

- ☐ _____
- ☐ _____
- ☐ _____
- ☐ _____

GOALS FOR MY BODY:

- ☐ _____
- ☐ _____
- ☐ _____
- ☐ _____

REMINDER

MY NOTE

PLANNER

MONTH: ....

YEAR: ....

MY TOP PRIORITIES

GOALS FOR
MY MIND:

- _____
- _____
- _____
- _____

GOALS FOR
MY BODY:

- _____
- _____
- _____
- _____

REMINDER

MY NOTE

PLANNER

MONTH: ....

YEAR: ....

MY TOP PRIORITIES

GOALS FOR MY MIND:

- ▪ _____
- ▪ _____
- ▪ _____
- ▪ _____

GOALS FOR MY BODY:

- ▪ _____
- ▪ _____
- ▪ _____
- ▪ _____

REMINDER

MY NOTE

PLANNER

MONTH: ....

YEAR: ....

MY TOP PRIORITIES

GOALS FOR MY MIND:	GOALS FOR MY BODY:
■ _____	■ _____
■ _____	■ _____
■ _____	■ _____
■ _____	■ _____

REMINDER

MY NOTE

Self Care
PLANNER

MONTH: ....

YEAR: ....

MY TOP PRIORITIES

GOALS FOR MY MIND:

- _____
- _____
- _____
- _____

GOALS FOR MY BODY:

- _____
- _____
- _____
- _____

REMINDER

MY NOTE

PLANNER

MONTH: ....

YEAR: ....

MY TOP PRIORITIES

GOALS FOR
MY MIND:

- _____
- _____
- _____
- _____

GOALS FOR
MY BODY:

- _____
- _____
- _____
- _____

REMINDER

MY NOTE

PLANNER

MONTH: ....

YEAR: ....

MY TOP PRIORITIES

GOALS FOR MY MIND:

- ■ _____
- ■ _____
- ■ _____
- ■ _____

GOALS FOR MY BODY:

- ■ _____
- ■ _____
- ■ _____
- ■ _____

REMINDER

MY NOTE

PLANNER

MONTH: ....

YEAR: ....

MY TOP PRIORITIES

GOALS FOR MY MIND:	GOALS FOR MY BODY:
▪ _____	▪ _____
▪ _____	▪ _____
▪ _____	▪ _____
▪ _____	▪ _____

REMINDER

MY NOTE

PLANNER

MONTH: ....

YEAR: ....

MY TOP PRIORITIES

GOALS FOR MY MIND:

- ◻ _____
- ◻ _____
- ◻ _____
- ◻ _____

GOALS FOR MY BODY:

- ◻ _____
- ◻ _____
- ◻ _____
- ◻ _____

REMINDER

MY NOTE

PLANNER

MONTH: ....

YEAR: ....

MY TOP PRIORITIES

GOALS FOR MY MIND:

- ■ _____
- ■ _____
- ■ _____
- ■ _____

GOALS FOR MY BODY:

- ■ _____
- ■ _____
- ■ _____
- ■ _____

REMINDER

MY NOTE

PLANNER

MONTH: ....

YEAR: ....

MY TOP PRIORITIES

GOALS FOR MY MIND:

- _____
- _____
- _____
- _____

GOALS FOR MY BODY:

- _____
- _____
- _____
- _____

REMINDER

MY NOTE

PLANNER

MONTH: ....

YEAR: ....

MY TOP PRIORITIES

GOALS FOR
MY MIND:

- _____
- _____
- _____
- _____

GOALS FOR
MY BODY:

- _____
- _____
- _____
- _____

REMINDER

MY NOTE

PLANNER

MONTH: ....

YEAR: ....

MY TOP PRIORITIES

GOALS FOR MY MIND:

- ◾ _____
- ◾ _____
- ◾ _____
- ◾ _____

GOALS FOR MY BODY:

- ◾ _____
- ◾ _____
- ◾ _____
- ◾ _____

REMINDER

MY NOTE

PLANNER

MONTH: ....

YEAR: ....

MY TOP PRIORITIES

GOALS FOR
MY MIND:

- _____
- _____
- _____
- _____

GOALS FOR
MY BODY:

- _____
- _____
- _____
- _____

REMINDER

MY NOTE

PLANNER

MONTH: ....

YEAR: ....

MY TOP PRIORITIES

GOALS FOR MY MIND:

- ▢ _____
- ▢ _____
- ▢ _____
- ▢ _____

GOALS FOR MY BODY:

- ▢ _____
- ▢ _____
- ▢ _____
- ▢ _____

REMINDER

MY NOTE

PLANNER

MONTH: ....

YEAR: ....

MY TOP PRIORITIES

GOALS FOR MY MIND:

- _____
- _____
- _____
- _____

GOALS FOR MY BODY:

- _____
- _____
- _____
- _____

REMINDER

MY NOTE

PLANNER

MONTH: ....

YEAR: ....

MY TOP PRIORITIES

GOALS FOR MY MIND:

- ▪ _____
- ▪ _____
- ▪ _____
- ▪ _____

GOALS FOR MY BODY:

- ▪ _____
- ▪ _____
- ▪ _____
- ▪ _____

REMINDER

MY NOTE

PLANNER

MONTH: ....

YEAR: ....

MY TOP PRIORITIES

GOALS FOR MY MIND:

- _____
- _____
- _____
- _____

GOALS FOR MY BODY:

- _____
- _____
- _____
- _____

REMINDER

MY NOTE

PLANNER

MONTH: ....

YEAR: ....

MY TOP PRIORITIES

GOALS FOR MY MIND:

- _____
- _____
- _____
- _____

GOALS FOR MY BODY:

- _____
- _____
- _____
- _____

REMINDER

MY NOTE

PLANNER

MONTH: ....

YEAR: ....

MY TOP PRIORITIES

GOALS FOR
MY MIND:

- ☐ _____
- ☐ _____
- ☐ _____
- ☐ _____

GOALS FOR
MY BODY:

- ☐ _____
- ☐ _____
- ☐ _____
- ☐ _____

REMINDER

MY NOTE

 *Self Care*

PLANNER

MONTH: ....

YEAR: ....

MY TOP PRIORITIES

GOALS FOR MY MIND:

- ☐ _____
- ☐ _____
- ☐ _____
- ☐ _____

GOALS FOR MY BODY:

- ☐ _____
- ☐ _____
- ☐ _____
- ☐ _____

REMINDER

MY NOTE

PLANNER

MONTH: ....

YEAR: ....

MY TOP PRIORITIES

GOALS FOR
MY MIND:

- ☐ _____
- ☐ _____
- ☐ _____
- ☐ _____

GOALS FOR
MY BODY:

- ☐ _____
- ☐ _____
- ☐ _____
- ☐ _____

REMINDER

MY NOTE

PLANNER

MONTH: ....

YEAR: ....

MY TOP PRIORITIES

GOALS FOR MY MIND:

- ◼ _____
- ◼ _____
- ◼ _____
- ◼ _____

GOALS FOR MY BODY:

- ◼ _____
- ◼ _____
- ◼ _____
- ◼ _____

REMINDER

MY NOTE

INTENTION

MONTH: ....

YEAR: ....

PHYSICAL SELF CARE

....
....
....
....

EMOTIONAL SELF CARE

....
....
....
....

SPIRITUAL SELF CARE

....
....
....
....

SOCIAL SELF CARE

....
....
....
....

NOTE TO SELF:

INTENTION

MONTH: ....

YEAR: ....

PHYSICAL SELF CARE	EMOTIONAL SELF CARE
....	....
....	....
....	....
....	....

SPIRITUAL SELF CARE	SOCIAL SELF CARE
....	....
....	....
....	....
....	....

NOTE TO SELF:

 *Self Care*

INTENTION

MONTH: ....

YEAR: ....

PHYSICAL SELF CARE

....
....
....
....

EMOTIONAL SELF CARE

....
....
....
....

SPIRITUAL SELF CARE

....
....
....
....

SOCIAL SELF CARE

....
....
....
....

NOTE TO SELF:

INTENTION

MONTH: ....

YEAR: ....

PHYSICAL SELF CARE

....

....

....

....

EMOTIONAL SELF CARE

....

....

....

....

SPIRITUAL SELF CARE

....

....

....

....

SOCIAL SELF CARE

....

....

....

....

NOTE TO SELF:

 *Self Care*

INTENTION

MONTH: ....

YEAR: ....

PHYSICAL SELF CARE

....

....

....

....

EMOTIONAL SELF CARE

....

....

....

....

SPIRITUAL SELF CARE

....

....

....

....

SOCIAL SELF CARE

....

....

....

....

NOTE TO SELF:

Self Care
INTENTION

MONTH: ....

YEAR: ....

PHYSICAL SELF CARE

....

....

....

....

EMOTIONAL SELF CARE

....

....

....

....

SPIRITUAL SELF CARE

....

....

....

....

SOCIAL SELF CARE

....

....

....

....

NOTE TO SELF:

Self Care
INTENTION

MONTH: ....

YEAR: ....

PHYSICAL SELF CARE

....

....

....

....

EMOTIONAL SELF CARE

....

....

....

....

SPIRITUAL SELF CARE

....

....

....

....

SOCIAL SELF CARE

....

....

....

....

NOTE TO SELF:

Self Care
INTENTION

MONTH: ....

YEAR: ....

PHYSICAL SELF CARE

....
....
....

EMOTIONAL SELF CARE

....
....
....

SPIRITUAL SELF CARE

....
....
....

SOCIAL SELF CARE

....
....
....

NOTE TO SELF:

Self Care

INTENTION

MONTH: ....

YEAR: ....

PHYSICAL SELF CARE

....
....
....
....

EMOTIONAL SELF CARE

....
....
....
....

SPIRITUAL SELF CARE

....
....
....
....

SOCIAL SELF CARE

....
....
....
....

NOTE TO SELF:

INTENTION

MONTH: ....

YEAR: ....

PHYSICAL SELF CARE

....
....
....

EMOTIONAL SELF CARE

....
....
....

SPIRITUAL SELF CARE

....
....
....

SOCIAL SELF CARE

....
....
....

NOTE TO SELF:

 # INTENTION

MONTH: ....

YEAR: ....

PHYSICAL SELF CARE

....

....

....

....

EMOTIONAL SELF CARE

....

....

....

....

SPIRITUAL SELF CARE

....

....

....

....

SOCIAL SELF CARE

....

....

....

....

NOTE TO SELF:

Self Care
INTENTION

MONTH: ....

YEAR: ....

PHYSICAL SELF CARE

....
....
....
....

EMOTIONAL SELF CARE

....
....
....
....

SPIRITUAL SELF CARE

....
....
....
....

SOCIAL SELF CARE

....
....
....
....

NOTE TO SELF:

INTENTION

MONTH: ....

YEAR: ....

PHYSICAL SELF CARE

....

....

....

....

EMOTIONAL SELF CARE

....

....

....

....

SPIRITUAL SELF CARE

....

....

....

....

SOCIAL SELF CARE

....

....

....

....

NOTE TO SELF:

INTENTION

MONTH: ....

YEAR: ....

PHYSICAL SELF CARE

....

....

....

....

EMOTIONAL SELF CARE

....

....

....

....

SPIRITUAL SELF CARE

....

....

....

....

SOCIAL SELF CARE

....

....

....

....

NOTE TO SELF:

 *Self Care*

INTENTION

MONTH: ....

YEAR: ....

PHYSICAL SELF CARE

....

....

....

....

EMOTIONAL SELF CARE

....

....

....

....

SPIRITUAL SELF CARE

....

....

....

....

SOCIAL SELF CARE

....

....

....

....

NOTE TO SELF:

INTENTION

MONTH: ....

YEAR: ....

PHYSICAL SELF CARE

....

....

....

....

EMOTIONAL SELF CARE

....

....

....

....

SPIRITUAL SELF CARE

....

....

....

....

SOCIAL SELF CARE

....

....

....

....

NOTE TO SELF:

INTENTION

MONTH: ....

YEAR: ....

PHYSICAL SELF CARE

....

....

....

....

EMOTIONAL SELF CARE

....

....

....

....

SPIRITUAL SELF CARE

....

....

....

....

SOCIAL SELF CARE

....

....

....

....

NOTE TO SELF:

INTENTION

MONTH:

YEAR: ....

PHYSICAL SELF CARE

....
....
....
....

EMOTIONAL SELF CARE

....
....
....
....

SPIRITUAL SELF CARE

....
....
....
....

SOCIAL SELF CARE

....
....
....
....

NOTE TO SELF:

 *Self Care*
INTENTION

MONTH: ....

YEAR: ....

PHYSICAL SELF CARE

....
....
....
....

EMOTIONAL SELF CARE

....
....
....
....

SPIRITUAL SELF CARE

....
....
....
....

SOCIAL SELF CARE

....
....
....
....

NOTE TO SELF:

Self Care
INTENTION

MONTH: ....

YEAR: ....

PHYSICAL SELF CARE

....
....
....

EMOTIONAL SELF CARE

....
....
....

SPIRITUAL SELF CARE

....
....
....

SOCIAL SELF CARE

....
....
....

NOTE TO SELF:

JOURNAL

MONTH: ....

YEAR: ....

AFFIRMATIONS

I'M PROUD OF MY...

I'M GRATEFUL FOR...

NOTE TO SELF:

....

....

....

....

JOURNAL

MONTH: ....

YEAR: ....

AFFIRMATIONS

I'M PROUD OF MY...

I'M GRATEFUL FOR...

NOTE TO SELF:

....

....

....

....

JOURNAL

MONTH: ....

YEAR: ....

AFFIRMATIONS

I'M PROUD OF MY...

I'M GRATEFUL FOR...

NOTE TO SELF:

....

....

....

....

JOURNAL

MONTH: ....

YEAR: ....

AFFIRMATIONS

I'M PROUD OF MY...

I'M GRATEFUL FOR...

NOTE TO SELF:

....

....

....

....

JOURNAL

MONTH: ....

YEAR: ....

AFFIRMATIONS

I'M PROUD OF MY...

I'M GRATEFUL FOR...

NOTE TO SELF:

....

....

....

....

Weekly Schedule Planner

Date : _____

Monday	Tuesday	Wednesday

Thursday	Friday	Saturday

Note :

Weekly Schedule Planner

Date : _____

Monday	Tuesday	Wednesday

Thursday	Friday	Saturday

Note :

Weekly Schedule Planner

Date : _____

Monday	Tuesday	Wednesday

Thursday	Friday	Saturday

Note :

Weekly Schedule Planner

Date : _____

Monday	Tuesday	Wednesday

Thursday	Friday	Saturday

Note :

Weekly Schedule Planner

Date : _____

Monday	Tuesday	Wednesday

Thursday	Friday	Saturday

Note :

Weekly Schedule Planner

Date : _____

Monday	Tuesday	Wednesday

Thursday	Friday	Saturday

Note :

Weekly Schedule Planner

Date : _____

Monday	Tuesday	Wednesday

Thursday	Friday	Saturday

Note :

Weekly Schedule Planner

Date : _____

Monday	Tuesday	Wednesday

Thursday	Friday	Saturday

Note :

DAILY PLANNER

Date :

Things To Do

- [ ]
- [ ]
- [ ]
- [ ]
- [ ]
- [ ]

Today's Focus

Priorities

Reminder

Note

TO DO LIST

Date :

Morning Tasks

-
-
-

Afternoon Tasks

-
-
-

Evening Tasks

-
-
-

TO DO LIST

Date :

Morning Tasks

- [ ]
- [ ]
- [ ]

Afternoon Tasks

- [ ]
- [ ]
- [ ]

Evening Tasks

- [ ]
- [ ]
- [ ]

TO DO LIST

Date :

Morning Tasks

- [ ]
- [ ]
- [ ]

Afternoon Tasks

- [ ]
- [ ]
- [ ]

Evening Tasks

- [ ]
- [ ]
- [ ]

TO DO LIST

Date :

Morning Tasks

- [ ]
- [ ]
- [ ]

Afternoon Tasks

- [ ]
- [ ]
- [ ]

Evening Tasks

- [ ]
- [ ]
- [ ]

TO DO LIST

Date :

Morning Tasks

- [ ]
- [ ]
- [ ]

Afternoon Tasks

- [ ]
- [ ]
- [ ]

Evening Tasks

- [ ]
- [ ]
- [ ]

TO DO LIST

Date :

Morning Tasks

- ☐
- ☐
- ☐

Afternoon Tasks

- ☐
- ☐
- ☐

Evening Tasks

- ☐
- ☐
- ☐

TO DO LIST

Date :

Morning Tasks

- [ ]
- [ ]
- [ ]

Afternoon Tasks

- [ ]
- [ ]
- [ ]

Evening Tasks

- [ ]
- [ ]
- [ ]

DAILY JOURNAL

Date :

DAILY JOURNAL

Date :

DAILY JOURNAL

Date :

DAILY JOURNAL

Date :

DAILY JOURNAL

Date :

DAILY JOURNAL

Date :

Daily Plan

To Do List

1. _____
2. _____
3. _____
4. _____
5. _____

Reminders for Today

_____

_____

_____

_____

_____

Schedule

8:00 AM

9:00 AM

10:00 AM

11:00 AM

12:00 PM

1:00 PM

2:00 PM

3:00 PM

4:00 PM

5:00 PM

6:00 PM

For Tomorrow

Notes

Daily Plan

To Do List

1. _____
2. _____
3. _____
4. _____
5. _____

Reminders for Today

_____
_____
_____
_____
_____

Schedule

8:00 AM

9:00 AM

10:00 AM

11:00 AM

12:00 PM

1:00 PM

2:00 PM

3:00 PM

4:00 PM

5:00 PM

6:00 PM

For Tomorrow

Notes

Daily Plan

To Do List

1. _____

2. _____

3. _____

4. _____

5. _____

Reminders for Today

_____

_____

_____

_____

Schedule

8:00 AM

9:00 AM

10:00 AM

11:00 AM

12:00 PM

1:00 PM

2:00 PM

3:00 PM

4:00 PM

5:00 PM

6:00 PM

For Tomorrow

Notes